Through the
Waspmouth
I Drew You

Essential Poets Series 285

Canada Council
for the Arts

Conseil des Arts
du Canada

ONTARIO ARTS COUNCIL
CONSEIL DES ARTS DE L'ONTARIO

an Ontario government agency
un organisme du gouvernement de l'Ontario

Canadä

Guernica Editions Inc. acknowledges the support of the Canada
Council for the Arts and the Ontario Arts Council.
The Ontario Arts Council is an agency of the Government of Ontario.

We acknowledge the financial support of the Government of Canada.

Nicola Vulpe

Through the Waspmouth I Drew You

GUERNICA EDITIONS
TORONTO · CHICAGO ·
BUFFALO · LANCASTER (U.K.)
2021

Elana Wolff, editor
Michael Mirolla, general editor
David Moratto, cover and interior design
Leonor Vulpe Albari, cover art: Abstract Green #10
Guernica Editions Inc.
287 Templemead Dr., Hamilton, Ontario, Canada L8W 2W4,
2250 Military Road, Tonawanda, N.Y. 14150-6000 U.S.A.
www.guernicaeditions.com

Distributors:
Independent Publishers Group (IPG)
600 North Pulaski Road, Chicago IL 60624
University of Toronto Press Distribution,
5201 Dufferin Street, Toronto (ON), Canada M3H 5T8
Gazelle Book Services, White Cross Mills
High Town, Lancaster LA1 4XS U.K.

First edition.
Printed in Canada.

Legal Deposit—First Quarter
Library of Congress Catalog Card Number: 2020948000
Library and Archives Canada Cataloguing in Publication
Title: Through the waspmouth I drew you / Nicola Vulpe.
Names: Vulpe, Nicola, 1954- author.
Series: Essential poets ; 285.
Description: First edition. |
Series statement: Essential poets series ; 285 | Poems.
Identifiers: Canadiana 20200362046 | ISBN 9781771835916 (softcover)
Classification: LCC PS8593.U55 T47 2021 | DDC C811/.54—dc23

for Maha
for Leonor

I

Ask the crested parrot.
She's partial to words,
and extravagant
in the solitude and sorrow
of exile.

*

On the seventh day the Lord
wrote poetry.
"Some rest!" he said
to the empty page.

II

Count back across the still sea,
back before the horizon slipped,
those short, furious years, galestruck,
shivering beneath the blackheaped sky.

*

Requiring no meaning, the previous labours
were trivial.

III

Drivelstring, syllablemush, clearquivering mucous,
I drew you across this yellow afternoon,
I hung you on white moonhorns.

I drew you through, into the eveningblue.
No one saw the spiderspunstrings I used.
No one heard the clicking instruments,
the hammerthuds, needlestitches, the
wheelwhirrings, pistonsneezes.

No one smelled the pumiceoil, or knew
why the mustardday, or where, suddenly,
the silvermoonsliver on which it hung
had gone. Or why.

IV

What about the eels, Heraclitus,
the fish, the long green weeds?
What about the sand, the swirling silt?

What about us, Heraclitus,
the watermites and the worms,
the dull, the uninspiring,

born into the dark river,
who die without crossing?

V

Bluecrow, Bluecrow,
Ink dries in the pen.

VI

Wait! Wait for that threadthinmoon to fill,
perigree bloodbloatthing that rolls,
rolls,across rooftops, that pulls
the ancientrootstem, the knotbind
algebra of dreams, of dimbeginnings,
the pulledfromtidefoam whimper.

Wait, just wait.
The poem will write itself.

VII

I deny you, blatherskites,
I deny you, doubtseeders, dreameaters,
selfimportant refuserakes.

VIII

Our cell doors were ajar,
someone had thrown open the gates.
Every night, every morning
we'd prayed for exactly this.

Rain had come at last.
Now we mill about the muddy yard,
we ponder the high walls,
the wires above, with their knives,
the iron gates askew on their hinges.

And from these gates we peer
into the terrifying mist beyond.

IX

The parrot blinks, blinks and asks for an orange.
Of course, of course, bluecrowparrot:
unrhymable orange, gurgledervish.

*

Will this small shell suffice, will this burrow?
The darkness hold when the great trees flame?

X

Browneyed, blueeyed, why are you surprised?
Berubbledconcrete, openwall, pinkslipper,
roomlessgreenchair, yellowbag.

I'm thirsty, I'm thirsty.

In the mudstreet, silent rattlebuckets collect puffsnow,
the greysky sleeps undreaming, thunderless.
No oilrage, no cloudclap,
no screetchbellow, cowlow,
no sheepbleet,
no caw.

*

Our phones, our laptops
had long ago failed.
The old radio was the last to conclude,
a few words no one understood,
then grey crackling.

The snow continued.
We made black tea on the stove.
"I'm hungry," said a child.

XI

Ah, parrot, pinkparrot, how do we answer?

*

The stone, the sky, the seed.
Indifferent as angels.

XII

Horizonsmudge, east-by-southeast.

*

Bluecrow, bluecrow,
pinkparrot in your mouth.

XIII

I name, I name. I name, I name, I name.
Nothing from nothing from nothing.
Clockthunk, clockthunk, glong, glong, clockthunk, glong,
slowday, midday, mudday, molassesday,
clay.

*

These my minutes, these my hours,
this my Parmenedian day, Parmenedian breath.

Obstinate, unmovingsun, the horizon awaits,
unmovingsoul, the earthdoors await.

Noisomenags, spiritcripplers, why thus?
Woundticklers, saltrubbers!

Why?

XIV

I counted the atomclouds, the electronsmudgespins,
I counted the quarkwaves, the imprecise,
laid out through the mistvague, a greyfreighted rule,
I rodmeasured the unhorizoned white, the angry
    rectangle,
immaculate jeerwhistle prisonsheet.

*

We no less than stars
suffer the whims of Einstein's laws.

Observe how some end:
a jet of light, a stone hurled
through cold space to earth—

Or linger on, and on,
half-lives halved,
and halved and halved again.

XV

Where the pulseflesh, inextricable pound?
Where the tortured lump, the achingvoiced
hollowing instrument, the philosopher's bane?

Like rainwater gone.
Rainwater gone,
to indifferent sea.

XVI

We know no season but our own,
our fish this, our fish that, our fish here,
our fish infinitepresent,
unarrowed moment, unweighted, undreamt,
in our tonguethick wrappingelement,
in our roofed darkjar, our unblinking now.

XVII

This morning, the cobwebbed seaslips,
the algebral leftovers, the vectorbreaks.
This morning, the stunted equation,
unfocused parabola, the withered sequence,
the undimensioned thread,
unreaching, scuttered out,
expired, but not quite, not quite.

XVIII

Through the waspmouth I drew these words,
waspfoottapped across glasssilence, rang
at each markpoint the empty bell, and drank
the browndullreward, the sandfilled cup
of everything, of all that is written
and to be written.

✳

When the Lord said,
"Let there be light"
He also set out,
like jumbled river stones
for us to stumble across,
all the shadows in between.

XIX

How? How do I fashion
from dullthinking soundbrick,
thornwearing syllogism, how,
clearedged inklines to draw you too, my lover,
from the whalebelly, the deadfeeding trench,
out through the waspmouth,
out through the cracked seed, the shrinking mote?

XX

Crowbeak curr, foxhead bird,
from wrinkled germ into light,
we pull roundbeast and fledgling alike,
talonfoot, pinkhand and wing.
None will suffice.
Scalelipped maw, spitting.

Heap them as they arrive, heap them,
feverbegotten, loampiercing asparaguspokes,
skyclimbing limbknots, green, green, green,
airloving grasps.

Heap them, heap them as they arrive,
unclassed, unsifted, unreasoned.

*

It's so nice to be wanted.

Except, perhaps,
by the police,

especially secret.

XXI

Graniteheaded mudburrowers,
pampabounding shinlegs, windlifted kites,
iceliving furchokes, monkeymimics,
sputtering logophagi all,
thrown before the whitewigged court.

They roar their innocence,
guiltless, they claim, because unknowing.

*

Can you claim such a defence?

XXII

Bluecrow, bluecrow,
pinkparrot again in your mouth.

XXIII

Now through the dusttomes, the larded pageslabs,
now through the sevenstone, the leatherwrapped,
the heftthumped sheafs, catcough furspews.

There's an answer, there is!

XXIV

In the unpondered fistswing, the unmeasured ragepit,
here, where pinkinnocence is funnelrammed,
bluntpushed through the softlipped mouth,
here, where the failedboxer and his knife,
his alligator clips, his blindsalt instruments,
the bludgeonwhip, the fourelement ingenuities.

Here, howldamp, the prisoner gasps.

So stipulates the law.

*

The syllogism stands.
Accept the premise, accept the conclusion.
All thought tends towards systems.

So rumbles the Königsberg scaffold.

XXV

There's an answer here, there is!

XXVI

The judges throw off their coiffes,
wrigglewalking sentence denied.
"Champagne!" calls the one, "champagne!"

The question is ended, the ironscream
no more, the instruments are broken.

*

Don't ask the weeds.
We're not given to introspect.
Why am I? Why indeed!
I scrabble for my bit of earth.
Unwanted, illformed,
I fear the hoe and spade,
care nothing for your roses.
The sun's half done,
and we're still arguing.

And will still, I suppose,
until in its crowd of stars our little light
sputters like a damp match

and goes cold.

XXVII

Gapemouthed, malmseyadled mooncalf,
what shadows did you see under the door's yellow
  seeplight?
What yawping wordruins rubcrawled through,
what nosewrinkling whether-but-if-then
pulled its toadwarted self into your soundholes?

*

The maddermatted lefthand, dishragstopped,
the windweeping snow,
a halfperfect number, unwordable,
fogslipped into the aeons.

What slatwort ashstorm burelslapped your eyes?
What eareating ambrein tickled your bloodsurfeited
  stiffleg?

XXVIII

Ask the parrot,
a poem begins with a word,
just one, my pinkcrested friend,
just one will do.

XXIX

Where is that bird?

XXX

I turn to the Icelandic poets,
they knew how to sail.

But no, not the blondehair ancients,
not the skalds, axethrowlouts, the Godscourges,
not they, dropjawed before shimmering abaculi,
not they, meadcupthumpers.

No, the moderns, they who write about gardens,
they whose pretty curtains frame life,
whose windwhipped flowers inspire.

*

Or maybe the Atom Poets,
they stopped by on Sunday for tea.

*

They're lying, of course.
I've seen the windrotten place:
a singular puffindot
sleetpushed skyward.

XXXI

The Leader shouts across his microphones.

XXXII

It always begins thus. The tyrant's head
drips on a pike in the square. Rain, mud.
Men fire Kalishnikovs into the air,
girls pull off their bright scarves and join the dance.

Weddings are promised. Those who had fled decide
to return. And from that old book buried
for years, a child's voice sounds out the sentence:
Who among the fearful will now command?

XXXIII

The parrot's come back to us,
pink and white, grey feet.

Where has she been?

XXXIV

I count, I count.
The olivemountain unsighted,
the ark bursts its waterswollen ribs.

I count, I count. I count.
Wraiths all. Wraiths all that entered.

XXXV

No word, still no word, not one word, no word.

*

Somewhere in the silt,
it's there, I know it.
We all do.

Beneath the clear, cold river,
we drown,
searching.

XXXVI

Bluecrow, bluecrow, pinkparrot in your mouth.

XXXVII

Note the cereusbloom,
celerygreenwhite, saffronpistils,
honeywink mouth,
gapesufficient to snaptrap a bat.

XXXVIII

I have adzscraped every page, razorsquiggled every line.
I have unstrung, restrung, unstrung,
restrung, unstrung, unstrung,
tangled every wrigglingsyllableheap,
ironmeasured, chromegauged
every foggrown notion, distilled, ethered and spindled,
pulled from darkthink cragtraps, longdiscontinuity
    drillholes.

Sanskritseeded, Greekgrown, Aramaicarabesque,
the joke's not done.

XXXIX

Pepper this, says the pinkparrot.
Profane that, she insists, pinkpepper
your longwinding, snakerootpath.

*

Trees are burdened, always.
Since the start of time, burdened.

XL

Ah, pinkparrot, pink parrot.
When I need you, pindropsilence.

XLI

Did you tear out the clouds?
Why did you tear out the clouds?
They were good clouds, comfortable.

Through the flappingrent, air evades us,
light too hisses out.

Look, the gash grows,
a tear has reached the horizon,
another cuts through the sun.

XLII

Osip's beast swells above,
the ancientbloatworm descends
through the tornballoon skywound,
with the uptorrent screet,
the sibilantlight flees.

The beast folds its unfeathered wings, squeezewriggles
its newtwhitebelly through.

The clouds lie shattered, the sun moans,
light wheezes through the widening,
airhollow screams, tinhowls.

*

Dandelionpuff, milkweedsatin rush,
lucentwinged thrumarmoured clankbeetle,
chitintubed legspurs, spindled splitswirlbits,
through the flapping gash, through the cracking scableak,
the tornboughs, the shattered treesplits, ashbricks, the
    boulders,
the lichentop stones, the wormwarm, sanddust,
coralfooted palms, achinggilled fish, seaslugs,
    mudwallowers, all
widdershinswhorl through the tremblingedged cut.
Why did you tear out the clouds?
The sky crumples, the beastflesh settles on our mouths.

Osip, why this beast?
This proteus, grottenolm, this molch?
This writhingpulled, bloodpinked, this lucentskinned
cavestreamspewed firepassing legworm?
Osip? this age? our age?

XLIII

The Leader shouts across his microphones.

XLIV

Sludgeslurp forth, slipperthrough slopcarpet,
thus we begin afresh, you, my bellydark, and me,
molluskscented compromise, you, my tripeburning
    gutcoal,
and me, gelatinsgloob on the cabbageleaf.

The mollusk has passed, such is tomorrow.

XLV

Spring, lightbringing season, season of promise,
season of sunwatered ice, of snowdraining gutters,
season of sudden poochgifts,
the pinktruth of appleflowers.

Such is our tomorrow.

XLVI

This, the machinery of my defeat, I erected
in the nosetickled morning, on the ammoniayellow
    dewfrost
one windpushed Sunday.

Under upturned shipribs, one. Yes, one only,
pewdrowsing misshaven rumplecoat. Furnace pipes
    rattlethump.

I've seen you before, says the pulpit.
Every raincold Sunday, every sleetmurdered November
    Sunday,
you, you wetsleep here on the sweatworn benchwood,
slothfaced, walleyed, earless.

XLVII

Says the pulpit, God's soapbox, God's slitherwhisper,
grind, grind your rubstone strungsyllables,
grind the gossamersouls,
the arachnidthreaded confusions of youth,
the tooworn, beigedrowned drones,
grind the brittleaged gravestarers, grind,
grind especially the greenwhite,
the porcelain, sundreaming leaf.

XLVIII

The world is your quernstone, Lord,
and we your corn.

*

¡No pasarán! ¡No pasarán!
Always we proclaim,
¡No pasarán!

But they do, my love.
They always do.

XLIX

The sundreaming leaf, pinkparrot,
will to woad and madder and weld turn,
and brickledry, to dust.

*

And, yes, I'd forgotten the language of plants.
Of course I had, and the geometry of animals.

I'd forgotten the algebra of stones, the calculus of
        mountains.
I'd forgotten the mouldcurses, the planktondrawls,
the amoebaciphers, the brushswish of sand,
the plunkpop of oceans,
their wortborn cousins, their fissurecradled peaseasoup,
the coldburinned lake, brightgushing feedrivers,
forgotten the lowdrone planetwhistles, the chiseletched,
the fractal screechspin of the stars' tumbleflights.

I'd forgotten them all, the photon slurpdrool,
the tinytwinkling atomburr twaddlewaltzes.
Gone!

Even the tick, tick, tick of my own danklonging.

Only the icegrowl scraping,
the freight of lava and lodestone.

L

Sylvia, Queen of Solipsistia, I disagree.
I open my eyes, a world bursts forth.
I close them, a world bursts forth.

Not funny, says Sylvia. Behind my eyes,
a lightless cave, a soundless hollow.

*

Answers Plato, in a pub of course,
My dears, I did not claim
it would be pretty.

LI

Leadlump, slurryfoot, flush!
Thus begins another undissembled day:
Formica, linoleum, aluminium, *a-loo-mí-nee-yum*,
coffee, coffee, click.

The radio rattles on about the war.

*

Last night we endured,
we endured the bombs, we endured
your Polonius counsel,
today, your treaclepaper condolences.

LII

We are weary.
The bluecrow sings tuneless to its chicks,
the pinkparrot considers the mirror.
Somewhere, far away, a dog whimpers.

*

Indeed we are weary.

LIII

I will draw you now,
now through the speckled foramina,
through the ethmoid plate, the sieve.
I will run you along braidpulled nervestrings,
frayed through the waspmouth clicking,
through from the worldclang and crash
through into the clotting darkness, behind the eyes
where the mildewing light nevercan
touch.

*

And Gilgamesh waited with pale Enkidu
until the worm dropped from his nose.

LIV

Time's snout wetsnuffles in.

Have you seen the yellowtooth cur?
How it leapt upon the morning, slavering?
Its frothjowls shook, its flanks trembled,
it howled into the pumpkinmoon.

Take this pen, write without enmity.
Its breath in your ear, write what you hear it speak.

LV

At day's blindend I waited for you,
I stood by a ravencold window, the snow
whisperclattered across the crackleleaves, the streetlight
    hummed.

I waited by the burntmirror glass, the snow
catrubbed the brickcold walls,
the wind queried the icepainted leaves,
tickled the liftproperties of watercrystal,
washed across orange treeshorn,
counted and recounted the absolute dragvalue of twig.

*

At day's blindend, by that ravencold window,
I toothmuttered back to myself.
It was a slippery accounting that followed,
some gallexcreted humour
prettysniff sprinkled with rosewater and jasmine.

*

At days's blindend,
time's snotdamp snout at last backsmacked a blink,
and I returned to you, all instruments agleam.

And you gave me to draw, for my longmonth's drear,
you gave me to hoist past hissclicking mandibles,
you gave me to draw through the pollensuckling
    feathermouth,
for one blinkpause only,
the narrowpointed, unbratticed conclusion
of my thousand coalsteeped hours.

⁕

Punchdrunk I leapt into you, cephalopod.
And your gidsinging colourclanged silent.

LVI

Thistlemouth, goopgluedeyes sleepsquint.
Ah, this headvault, this chalkstone hollow,
Ah, this clamoozed, this woolrheumed ragcavity.

Zinclightflakes sift,
the window is blue, the stifftentacled tree beyond,
empty.

LVII

Peevish cistern, vengeful clay,
through whitedry Bactria, drier Turan,
I brickfoot, I ploodstrag, I raglump.

Whirlfunnels rise, stonegrit, bonedust.
The camels lopsway and halt, their eyelashes fill.

*

This was the map they used, the *Kitay-kharita*.
So said the Damascus geographer, all the wells are marked.
Darius followed it into Scythia, Thomas Nasrani to
    Kerala,
And the Great Khan himself rode its shaded avenues to
    Paris,
maybe even La Vérendrye to the golden mountains,
and the islands of the edge of the world.

*

All the angeled wells are marked, every greendarkened
    lee.
The Great Khan himself, the Great Khan ...
ate his own tongue.

The stonefilled wells laughed at his silks,
his jadewhite rings and his scrolls. The Great Khan
drank his last inkdrop, slaughtered his horse.

The targloop blood sandscuttled into the lanterned night,
the Great Khan ate his claynettled tongue.

LVIII

I looked for you, true heart,
in finegrainnailgrime and greygritted navelleavings,
in my eternal evermutable lensecorner,
in the woolpeppers, sweaterfurfleas twiggling,
in the filigreed, the tuaregblued handback tessellates.

LIX

The angeled wells of course were empty.

LX

This stoppedbreath day shadowpulls, nightinches.

LXI

Geographer! Geomancer more like,
sixteensided liemill, elementfrauding alchemist,
alembicboiler, chimerabreeder. Hermeticist, algebrist!

LXII

My tongue blackswells. The mudpan cells edgecurl,
the bakedslur riverfloor crimbles, the weldarc sky aches,
pales, pales against its own eggrobinblue.
Across shadowedless flat, threadthin fishribs
heatshiver, silvergrass meadowhints,
gleaming parchcrystal patches wait. From barenorth
saltdrifts advance.

LXIII

This the dewbelly scaleworm,
this the nakedwing wrogglegiant,
this the beast, dead, dead, dead.

LXIV

Not dead.

LXV

I began with hempcord and wirelash,
I hooked the nearpink bloatgut. It yawed
and rolled, pitched, windmurdered airfish,
its skinwings thrashed, its spitsplashed jowls
loosejiggled. It quaked, it crawed.

The clouds rose, it passed beneath,
so close we smelled its pussing junebuggut.
I crotched each thousandleg,
wirewound each bloodweeping notch,
stumpfixed, stonetethered the steelbristle forest.

The umbelliferous clouds rose, the beast
passed beneath, the beast shrieked, slammed
its wings and sloughed. The clouds cracked.
The night, the starless night burst through,
the beast was free. Somewhere beneath us,
a cowlow faded under the wind.

LXVI

Raincolumn strikes the river,
slate and pounding.

*

I saw this at sea once, the column, the boat.
We dipped behind a wave, bobbed back,
and the boat was gone.

We were alone, my love. We were alone.

LXVII

Stoke, stoke, stoke the dreamfurnace,
the katydid lemongreens fizzle on the neon,
droptwirlly to the tarmac.

The moon does not move, the sun refuses to rise.

Stoke, stoke, stoke the orangewelt,
this locustdark vault closes.

My crinklepaper, greyknot skeinveins—etherless!
Etherless as the eternal clockpound, the distant
    fridgemumble,
etherless as the neonfizzle, the tarmack twirllycrack.

LXVIII

Eliot's stinkpurples push through cold earthshell,
the parsniptoothed curr has reached its end,
it huskycurls its nose under its featherfrayed tail,
it knows the wetday has settled, it knows
the lettucehopes, the greenheaded wormstalks won.

LXIX

Green is the number 3, π the silver divining rod,
e the winedark water. Irrationals, fearless, chestthumpingly
    grey,
imperfect 5, some wet, hirudinunstopped brown.
2, the empty colour of tears. 1, every redgashed birth,
every prime of course, also red, infinitenuanced,
ochre to scarlet, sienna to crimson, vermillion,
    vermillion.
Vermillion, the velvetplushbristles of my cordgnawing
    wait.

LXX

I riverstonestepped the fibonaccis, algaeslippery as
    troutskin,
I wettoed their cellardamp domes. The blackneedle
    spruce
leaned madly, their granitewedged fingers lewdprodding
mossed earth, clamping lumpgrey,
defeatscattered glacierleavings, black erratics.

*

The tornribbon whitenarrow sky, cloudwash and
    lakevapour,
returns to the question:
Would I sliptrip, would I not?

LXXI

I galamseyered the thicksmeared dross, the rubble,
I reeved through the icewrapped shade.
Under the windshook branches,
the climbing fibonaccis nagpulled my elbow,
my tickfed shivering.

LXXII

And 0, of course. 0, the whistlehymn of ghosts.

LXXIII

I outslunk earthlong from the mossed yearday,
but the houleswell rose to meet me,
the morktoothed curr would not sleep.

LXXIV

Call the crested parrot.
She blinks,
and turns away.

LXXV

Why this flapdoodle, this keening catgut wassail?
Why this fervid hokum, untrue as a Saskatchewan
    sundog?
Armslip again your grogramshirtitch and blackkerchief
    lament.

Footslop, sloopfot, flootsop, pootflot, sot.
Rooddrag this stationless thornsweep,
footslop, sloopfot, flootsop, pootflot, sot.
But you're skint, slagrid,
you're cockcrowthrice, splooshmuffled, wrapped.

*

Copperbottomed prophecy coaxes the floatingbeast.
The cocolitzli tugs its cloudmoorings,
its blackgleam chains, its coilwire.
Will it sloopforward—drossladen, sloughborn firedamp?
Or marlinleap through the sun, rub the waterfoamed
    morning?

*

The narrowhand leadshudders forward, the clock closes in,
the scops maunder squashily on.

Spumebores push the blackstone shore, squirlsloop
the skerriedcoves where we threw, unthinking,
our tares.

*

They returned, laden of course, those tares.

*

Our careened shiphulks,
we left where teetering chance had pushed them,
and we ran.

LXXVI

Do you remember, Parvaneh?
You asked me if Persian girls are beautiful.
You were married, Parvaneh,
as was I.

*

We invent precise taxonomies, they do not suffice.

LXXVII

Straddle it!

They're lazy things,
need to be primed,
deceitful.

LXXVIII

Indeed, we fleajumped into tomorrow.
Heaving dampskank, dewlipped muskheaven,
the ant could not evade the fire,
nor the colourrain that came afterwards, relentless,
the tourmalinesea, the greensea, the malachite,
    wineshadowed,
the drunken, the nightsea, the empty reddisk.

*

You forbade me sleep,
but morning came anyway.

*

We opened our eyes, and we listened.

*

These were the lies we told ourselves,
the lies so we could keep our hearts open
just a few hours more.

LXXIX

Through the waspmouth I drew you,
the antthroat, the honeymaker beegut,
I drew you through the needleeye,
swaying baubleship, thirstless bloat, camel.

I drew you from the sandholedrag,
I drew you with your heaving treasure,
I drew you, eyefilled, lipcracked, choked.

*

The thoughtthrow stumbles,
falls to the gravelpath,
dustblurred, the path
washes into sandcloud.

LXXX

The ink dries in the pen.

LXXXI

We talked until the sky surprised us,
the open window, the birds suddenly a racket,
beyond, the growing thrum.
So soon, we thought, so soon.

Imagine Akureyri,
the horizon awash at last,
blue not indigo, eggyellow, carmine,
then night again, then night.

Such weariness, conversation.

Such weariness.

LXXXII

A wormturn under the loesscrumble,
a poke through the snowfed wet.
The stickyleafed morning recedes.
A goatlaugh. I begin to dig. No one.
No one. No, no one ticklesniffs, no one twitchflares,
no one mutebutton pauses. No.
No one pokes the soundsheetvelour, the courseknitted
    hum,
No one pulls the brownpapered nightweight.
No one, certainly, backsteps, whipsaws and statues.

*

Gone the boilblood, gone the icevein, gone
the nightwhorl, the benthtumble hurl.
Gone my wordseeding coalfog, my sulphic, lampsnuffing,
my ghoulvapour amici.

*

I dig, I dig. I dig. Malmsey and mallow and canesyrup tea,
fingercounted te-dum, te-dum. Where the rusty
    cardoorscrape?
where the windbuckled zincsheet, the carbuncle?
where the spinfire, the cinnabar, the skullshaking,
loinbursting howl?

I dig, I dig, I shovelsweep, drysieve, sift.
Under clawroot and stone, I pickscratch, I pound.

My sweatthank wage?—potter's rotlung.
Glooptrod lavender, redolent wickpetal, cinnamony.
Bergamotstained brown thinswill,
and on the cuplip a spoonbell.

LXXIII

I beg you, I beg you, if I cannot,
then whitedamp, alabaster mute.

*

... or in the stars.
Let's say that's where we'll end,
the jewelled night.

This will comfort us, knowing.
Cold as the journey might become,
or long.

LXXXIV

Flipswitch, blink. Fluolightblast,
roachfoot twittle, thumbsize brownblacks
scurryslide troodle through the fridgecrack greasegrill.

*

In this city of snow and the mute,
I have measured every sidewalk
with footsteps and longing.

LXXXV

Parrot on her perch, sunforgotten,
moonstarwretched, exile: Why have you waked me?

LXXXVI

I meet Meursault on a beach:
Are you alone, says I?
I am now, answers Meursault.

*

Ffremydborn, ffremydburied.

LXXXVII

Rosyfingered, winedark?
In the Hadrumat perhaps, from barnacled Muscatquai,
into the Zanzibarsea, eyerubbing nacremirror.

133 degrees 76 minutes, a simple eternity,

LXXXVIII

Through the waspmouth I drew you,
knockbodied, glodlimbed mudlouts,
bonecreaked krakeneating churls.

Through hymenopteran night,
apocrital ink I threaded and tied,
I quipucounted, I knottallied,
notchreasoned, wallcut: barfivescratch,
barfive, barfive. Scratch, scratch.

Through the waspmouth I drew you,
and still the nacremirror, the dhowfloating
emerald, the far, far pelicanbay holds you.

LXXXIX

Heraclitus meets Parmenides by a river:

Make the river stop, says Heraclitus.
Stop what? answers Parmenides.

XC

*Some few of us remember
midsummer.*

*A story in an old book
about faraway countries,
distant peoples.*

XCI

Parmenides, Parmenides, overclever
witchthinker: now, not now?
Infinite, unmoving now.

XCII

Pinkparrot with your chain,
you dreamt. What dream was it took you from me?
What dream took you from yourself?

*

I found you hanged, one wing clasped,
the other brushing the floor. The window open,
the sun caressed the sill, openeyed you turned.

XCIII

I drew you across the broken sea,
an unsailed ship pitching, galefrayed halyards flapping,
the ship waverose then fell, the wavecrests closed.

I dragged you over parched riverstones,
over murkwhite flats. Timebleached, the earth
was silent—how could it not be?

*

I molescraped, I nosepushed through your sweetwarm
    remains,
turmeric hint, cinammon and kelp, the droolbubble
    wateredge
pushed up the sand, pulled back, pushed up again.

A tarhole rose where yesterday the moon had
    glowfloated,
some unknown crabbird cawcawed and swooped.

Pinkparrot, the sunpainted sill is mute,
the catkinbreeze cannot decide.

XCIV

Now the bluecrow determines to speak.
Ignore him, turn away.
He'll conjure up the wrangled nest,
the ink behind your eyes.

Crow, dog. Blue crow, black dog.

XCV

A word, a word, a word,
bloodhanged bluecrow, blackdogmouth.

*

I drew you into the earth.

*

At least we'll forever have now.

Now,
when the sidewalk swallows the sky,
when birds begin to howl,
and our tongues are turned to ash.

*

Bluecrow, bluecrow.

*

I should apologize.
I should, I know.
But the words,
the words I'd use,

they're as rightfully yours
as this air I breathe,
as the rough sand
on this grey shore.

XCVI

No comet streaks across the indigo.
No planetarc, no starcurve, comet.
Of course, no comet.

*

Silent parrot on her perch,
she stretches her wing and shifts,
opens her beak …
Or so did she once.

What use this word I've found at last?

Thrumming silence, childhood's dust,
grimy window, rain.

*

Switchflick into nightwait, airsink.

*

This, I suppose, is the end.
Though, again, under its trowelful of dirt
the worm will be wanting his lunch,
and the seed will push pale tendrils to the sun.

XCVII

At day's blindend, I timedredged and tallied
the slooparrived ragtonnage, sans tret, sans cloff.
At the zerosummed arrowstop, the barman's whistle,
the demurrage paid, suttleweight nul.

*

We walked until our feet bled,
we walked until the fences tore our rags,
we walked until the truncheonmen fell on us,
we walked until the sun set and the sun rose.

We walked until we remembered only
how once our feet bled, how once we had rags,
how our bones were broken,
until we remembered only
how once the sun set and the sun rose.

*

Thus we are free say the saints, thus
the conclusion lizards into us all.

*

Boatman, boatman, here is your coin.

XCVIII

Ink will not be affixed to air or wind.

*

Where are we now, so far from our homes?
What journey? No compass, no map, alone.

And the star we knew like a sister
has hidden itself amongst all the others.

XCIX

The sky tugs the last leaves,
the neighbour's playing Aznavour
again and again and again,

Triste Venise, triste Venise …

*

The neighbour's playing Fairouz,

'Aateeni alnaya wa gheni …
Give me the flute and sing …

A life is a line written … but only in water
                    … *lakin bi maa'*

The parrot's hanged, the bluecrow swollen.

*

And the sea received us.

Shimmering,
winedark, windtorn,

murdering sea.

Acknowledgements

I am grateful to the editors and publishers of the following magazines and books in which parts of *Through the Waspmouth I Drew You* have appeared:

    Alba: xiv

    Cinquefoil: xiv

    The Manhattan Review: iv, xxvi, xxxii, xlii, xliii

Special thanks to the staff at Guernica Editions, especially publishers Michael Mirolla and Connie McParland, assistant publisher Anna van Valkenburg, publicist Margo LaPierre, and my very patient and precise editor, Elana Wolff.

I am also immensely grateful to Mark Frutkin, Alison Hobbs, Rebecca Leaver, Seymour Mayne, Richard Owens, and Susan Robertson, who have given so much of their time and themselves to read and listen to this and other poems, offering their thoughtful criticism, wisdom, hospitality, and friendship.

Maha Albari and Leonor Vulpe Albari, my debt to you through all these years, for your counsel and your patience especially, is immeasurable.

About the Author

Nicola Vulpe was born in Montreal. He completed a doctorate in philosophy at the Sorbonne, and taught in Spain before settling in Ottawa. His poems have appeared in journals such as *Alba*, *The Antigonish Review*, *The Manhattan Review*, *Mediterranean Poetry*, *Slush Pile Magazine*, and *Stand Magazine*, and he has published a novella, *The Extraordinary Event of Pia H., who turned to admire a chicken on the Plaza Mayor*, as well as three collections of poetry, *When the Mongols Return*, *Blue Tile* and, also from Guernica, *Insult to the Brain*, which received the Fred Cogswell Award for Excellence in Poetry.

Untitled

by

Leonor Vulpe Albari

Abstract Green #10

by

Leonor Vulpe Albari

Printed in March 2021
by Gauvin Press,
Gatineau, Québec